becoming a woman **of influence**

a part of the THRIVE! *study series*

becoming a woman **of influence**

making a lasting impact on others

carol kent

Discipleship Inside Out™

NavPress is the publishing ministry of The Navigators, an international Christian organization and leader in personal spiritual development. NavPress is committed to helping people grow spiritually and enjoy lives of meaning and hope through personal and group resources that are biblically rooted, culturally relevant, and highly practical.

For a free catalog go to www.NavPress.com or call 1.800.366.7788 in the United States or 1.800.839.4769 in Canada.

ISBN-13: 978-1-57683-421-3

Cover design: David Carlson
Cover image: Ryan McVay/PhotoDisc and DigitalVision
Creative Team: Dan Rich, Karen Lee-Thorp, Darla Hightower, Glynese Northam
        Pat Reinheimer

Some of the anecdotal illustrations in this book are true to life and are included with the permission of the persons involved. All other illustrations are composites of real situations, and any resemblance to people living or dead is coincidental.

Unless otherwise identified, all Scripture quotations in this publication are taken from *The Message: New Testament with Psalms and Proverbs* by Eugene H. Peterson, copyright © 1993, 1994, 1995, used by permission of NavPress Publishing Group. Other versions include: the *Holy Bible, New International Version®* (NIV®). Copyright © 1973, 1978, 1984, 2011 by Biblica, Inc.® Used by permission of Zondervan. All rights reserved worldwide. www.zondervan.com. The "NIV" and "New International Version" are trademarks registered in the United States Patent and Trademark Office by Biblica, Inc.®

Printed in the United States of America

8 9 10 11 12 13 / 17 16 15 14 13

contents

read this first

" "Me? A woman of influence?" Maybe it sounds like an arrogant and improbable goal for your life. But the influence this book talks about has nothing to do with selfish pride or with impressing people. It has everything to do with shaping your heart to the image of Jesus Christ, with becoming a woman who practices the principles He modeled, and with influencing others to do the same.

This book is a condensed discussion guide based on *Becoming a Woman of Influence* by Carol Kent. It is designed to help small groups of women learn together how to become Christ-followers and influencers. You can use this book profitably on your own, but we encourage you to gather a friend or several friends to join you on the journey.

Chapter 1 introduces the theme of the book: how to influence people's lives as Jesus did. The next six chapters each explore a principle Jesus practiced when He influenced others. His influence was never arrogant or manipulative; it selflessly drew the best out of people. Your influence can do the same. At the end of each chapter you'll find discussion questions, Bible study questions, prayer ideas, and practical action steps — everything you need for a fun and fruitful discussion group.

To get the most out of your discussions, read each chapter before you meet as a group to discuss it. However, if your time for homework is limited, your group can agree to read portions of the chapter during your meeting.

We hope you enjoy discussing this book.

chapter one

impacting lives like jesus did

during our first few years of marriage, my husband, Gene, and I were youth directors in a church in Newaygo, Michigan. During the day Gene taught English and journalism in a public school, and I directed the alternative education program for pregnant teenagers. As director, I individualized curriculum so my students could stay in high school for the duration of their pregnancies. During my last year in the program, I had sixty-eight pregnant, unwed students. Seven of them were only fourteen years old.

I soon discovered something surprising. Teenage girls were hanging out in my office before and after school, talking to me about makeup, boys, babies, life, God, and their relationship struggles at home. The same thing was happening before, during, and after youth events at church. I was being asked all sorts of questions by these teens:

- "I'm a new Christian and I have some questions about the Bible. Can you help me?"
- "I can't get along with my mother and dad. We fight all the time. How can we talk if we can't quit yelling?"
- "When you fell in love, how did you know Gene was the man you were supposed to marry?"
- "How can you know God's will for your life? I'm a senior and I have to decide what I'm going to do next year. My parents are putting pressure on me to apply to a college and I don't know what to do."

- "I have a friend who needs God in her life, but I'm shy about talking about my faith. What would you say to her if you were me?"

Even though I believed I needed to find an older, more mature Christian woman who could teach me how to mentor others, I began to realize I was already having an impact. These teenagers were looking to me for wise counsel and practical advice. I had never thought of myself as an "influencer," but it seemed natural to build relationships with these girls and to offer solid biblical answers to their questions. I was in a position to influence, whether I felt ready or not!

EACH OF US IS AN INFLUENCER

Recently a young woman told me about her eleventh-grade math teacher. It was near the end of the year and Meghan McIntyre was feeling isolated and hurt, searching for a reason to live. She said, "I was closer to choosing death than life." Then Meghan asked this teacher to sign her yearbook. Unaware of Meghan's emotional state, he wrote:

"Consider the lilies of the field. They sow not neither do they spin. Yet Solomon, in all his glory was not arrayed like one of these." If God so clothes the grass of the field, shall He not much more clothe you, Meghan? You have been a source of joy to me. Thanks for all your help in the math department, and may you achieve your goals with joy.

MR. OTTLEY

Mr. Ottley's words, quickly jotted down in a high school yearbook, provided Meghan with warmth and with the hope that God might have something to offer her. She was incredulous that she had brought joy to someone else — or that someone might wish that *she* experience joy. Oh, how she wanted that very thing!

Mr. Ottley's words made Meghan curious — who was this God? Jesus commanded, "Go into all the world and preach the good news

Jesus commanded, "Go into all the world and preach the gospel to all creation" (Mark 16:15, NIV). Mr. Ottley had taken the time to put in writing the good news that God cared for Meghan. His mission field included the school where he taught — and he proclaimed the good news to her, a student in his calculus class who needed hope. His words prepared the way for Meghan's life-changing encounter with Christ. In her first year of university studies, other Christians came and watered the seed Mr. Ottley had planted, and Meghan finally experienced new life in Jesus.

Mr. Ottley had no idea how his words had affected Meghan until his retirement party years later. As the floor was opened for comments, Meghan told her story, looked Mr. Ottley in the eyes, and said, "Thank you for writing in the yearbook of my life." This man had unintentionally influenced Meghan to search for the most important answers in life. He had simply lived as a Christian teacher should live and responded to her in a Christlike way.

We all influence people, whether we recognize it or not. However, it wasn't until I experienced a significant birthday that I determined to be more intentional about how I was influencing others.

SHAPING HEARTS INTO HIS IMAGE

My decision to be more intentional about how I influenced others was prompted by a personal milestone: another "decade marker" birthday. I had approached it with dread and apprehension, and I wanted this birthday to pass with little fanfare. However, my friends had other ideas. On the evening of "the big day," Gene and I were invited to the home of friends. Upon arriving, we settled in for a night of great conversation. Suddenly there was a knock at the back door and in marched a room full of friends, many of whom I hadn't seen for a long time. Carrying black balloons and gag surprises, they sang "Happy Birthday," and the party began. Their gifts exercise videos, magazines for "retired folks," suggestions for menopausal madness, and laxatives. Lots of laxatives! We laughed, ate cake, remembered old times, and enjoyed the safety and security of relationships that had been forged over time.

The next day another gift arrived from a new friend, someone I had been mentoring by long distance. It was a book with these words inscribed inside the front cover: "Thank you for shaping my heart to His image." The words pierced my heart.

Over the next few months I received several notes from women with questions about God, parenting challenges, relationship struggles, job changes, and ministry choices. Many of these letters were from women who longed for a mentor. With each letter I became more certain that God wanted me to devote the last half of my life to influencing young leaders who would carry His work on to future generations. I could think of no better model to follow than Jesus, so I began to study His life and how He related to people. The Gospels tell us that Jesus poured His life into a few people, and in turn this small group impacted the world and all of history. We can't read Matthew, Mark, Luke, and John without coming across numerous examples of one-on-one encounters Jesus had with people — encounters that radically changed their lives.

One of my favorites is how Jesus interacted with Matthew, the tax-collector-turned-disciple. Jesus walked by Matthew's booth one day while he was on duty. There he was: a capable money handler, a leader, a man of authority and power . . . someone who might have skimmed some of the profits off the top. But Jesus saw Matthew with different eyes. He saw who Matthew could become — one of His biographers! He saw weaknesses that could be turned into strengths. He envisioned a transformed lifestyle. A new passion. A tenacious loyalty. As Jesus passed by, He called to Matthew, "Follow me." And Matthew did.

As I studied the life of Christ, I wanted to know more so that I could follow His example of how to influence people in ways that

would make a lasting difference. Once I had identified my purpose — studying how Jesus influenced lives, integrating those principles into my own life, and passing them on to the next
generation — I experienced a freedom I hadn't felt for a long time.
Always busy "doing," I often felt pulled in too many directions. I
now had an outstanding reason to say, "No, I won't be able to accept
that invitation because I am convinced God wants the concentration
of my energy in another direction." It became easy to quickly and
efficiently say yes to opportunities for ministry that were in line with
my mission to evangelize, equip, encourage, and empower people to
impact others with their God-given potential.

AN INVITATION TO AN ADVENTURE

What would happen if you decided to influence lives on purpose? I
want to challenge women to become more intentional about how we
influence others, not because we *have* to, but because we *want* to. Not
because it is our Christian obligation, but because it brings great
meaning and joy to our lives. Not because of *duty*, but because of *love*.
Let's be like Jesus. Let's be women of conviction and passion. Let's
intentionally influence other women because it is a high calling and
a part of our predesigned purpose.

I didn't write this book to make women feel like failures as
Christians if they have not made a lifetime commitment to mentor
a younger woman, nor did I write it to present this model as the cor-
rect way to mentor. The sole purpose of this book is to inspire and
equip women to impact lives as Jesus did. Many of us have dreamed
of having an older woman with whom we meet on a regular basis
who will point out our gifts and provide advice, encouragement, and
resources. Someone to give us wise counsel day or night, someone to
whom we can speak our mind and tell our secrets, knowing they will
be guarded carefully. Someone with whom to pray and dream. But
sad to say, this "idealistic dream" is usually far from reality.

As part of my research for this book, I designed a survey that I sent to almost one hundred Christian leaders. One question asked whether the person had had a lifetime mentor. To my surprise, only a handful of these gifted Christian leaders had one mentor for life. Almost without exception, the respondents talked of many people who had influenced them in positive and life-changing ways. Sometimes this occurred through a one-time encounter; at other times these mentors were influential for a period of time. A few of the individuals I surveyed said the person who had influenced them the most was a historical figure — obviously someone they had never even met!

As I've studied Christ's life, I've come up with six principles for impacting the lives of the people around us in profoundly meaningful ways. Whether we act as lifetime mentors, friends, encouragers, or seasonal mentors, we can embrace and pass on the principles Jesus lived by. They are powerful and purposeful illustrations of what mentoring is all about.

What would happen if we took Christ's example seriously? Even if the results were only a small percentage of what Jesus accomplished, the results would be remarkable. Jesus influenced individuals from a wide variety of educational and vocational backgrounds. Some were from dysfunctional families. A few were professionals; many were common laborers. Some were fearless, and others lacked courage. However, He saw in each the potential to become great leaders, and He inspired them to commit time and energy to learn from Him. He motivated them so much that they longed to be with Him, and even after He ascended into heaven, they carried on His work because they knew they would be with Him again.

Jesus' life gives us an example of how to live. His principles for influencing lives are timeless and, more than that, they are available for us to use today. Are we eager to discover what they are? Are we willing to be accountable for what we learn? Have we avoided the responsibility of mentoring others because we feel inadequate?

Jesus had only three years of public ministry, but the impact He had on those He mentored still influences you and me today. If you long to bring the essence of Jesus Christ into the space you occupy, if you desire to influence lives as Jesus did, if you are eager to live for something that will last forever, read on. Come and join me on this adventure!

1. If you don't already know the members of your group, please introduce yourself. Then think of one older person (outside your family) who has influenced your life in a positive, spiritually challenging way. Describe for the group what this person did to affect the direction of your life.

2. Reread the story of Meghan and her teacher, Mr. Ottley, on page 10. Carefully look at the inscription this influential teacher wrote in her high school yearbook. What in Mr. Ottley's words do you think gave Meghan so much hope and pointed her toward Christ?

3. The word *influence* has to do with a person's wisdom or force of character that makes a lasting impact on the behavior or choices of another person. Read Matthew 9:9-13.

   a. How did Jesus influence Matthew?

   b. Matthew began to influence his friends when he barely knew Jesus. How did he influence them?

c. What do you learn about Jesus' character and values from this passage?

4. In John 10:10, Jesus stated the purpose of His life: "I came so that they can have real and eternal life, more and better life than they ever dreamed of."

a. What are some of the ways Jesus gave people a better life when He walked on this earth?

b. How has Jesus impacted your life?

5. Read Matthew 5:13-16. Who do you know who lives as light in a dark world? What is it about that person that makes him or her a light?

6. What are some areas of your life in which you have the opportunity to be light in the world, or a source of influence (for example, with your children's friends or with coworkers)?

7. Take a moment on your own to review the following longings. Circle the ones with which you currently identify. Then share your responses with the group to the degree that you feel comfortable doing so.

- "I wish I had someone who would mentor me."

- "I long for accountability in a friendship with someone who has known the Lord longer than I have, but the people I know are so busy I don't know who to ask."

- "I wish I knew someone with whom I could share my dreams and who would listen and give me honest feedback."

- "I long to connect with a younger Christian woman who I could encourage, support, and challenge to be her best for Christ."

- "My marriage is less than I had hoped. I thought I was marrying the strong, silent type, but now I know I just married a man who doesn't know how to communicate. Who can I talk to without embarrassing my husband?"

- "My boss has been unfair. I'm not given the respect I should have for my position at work. I need this job, but I need to know how to confront my boss in an appropriate way. Who can I talk to?"

- "I'm a new Christian. I want to learn about the Bible and I long to know how to pray, but I need guidance. Do you know anybody who could work with me on my spiritual growth?"

- "I wish I had a younger woman in my life who would be interested in personal and spiritual growth. I long to help someone else through the hurdles I faced in earlier years."

8. How can this group pray for you? (For example, would you like prayer about one of the longings you marked above?)

One way you can make a difference in someone's life is simply by inviting her to join this group! Pause to think of the name of one person you could invite. Share these names with the group.

Take a few minutes to pray for one another, asking God to respond to the needs and longings of your hearts. Pray also for the women you want to invite to join this group and for opportunities to invite them.

chapter two

the principle of time alone with god

for years I raced from one meeting or activity to another because I hated being alone. I equated solitude with loneliness. It made me feel worthless and uncomfortable. To me, a productive life consisted of a full calendar and constant interaction. However, the more things I put into my schedule, the less happy I became. And there were times when I felt used by people I loved because the more I did, the more they expected me to do.

After our son, Jason Paul, was born, I decided to leave teaching and become a stay-at-home mom. That time was incredibly difficult for me. I loved my baby, but I missed feeling "important" as an award-winning teacher. One day I spent an afternoon with one of my mentors, and she spoke of looking forward to the next day because her calendar had *nothing* on it. She told me she regularly scheduled these open days in her life to spend a quiet day alone with God. She smiled when I asked what she could possibly find to do with Him . . . alone . . . *all day.*

She spent the rest of the afternoon telling me how she and God spent their days together. She talked as if God were her best friend. As I was about to leave, she told me, "My days with Him — especially when the interruptions are minimal — are my favorite days." I knew she meant it. I left excited about scheduling time alone with God. I knew I had a lot to learn, but this was a beginning.

I've come a long way since then, and I'm convinced that time alone with God is nonnegotiable if we want to be like Jesus and to influence others like He did.

What can we learn from Jesus about spending time alone with God?

IT WAS A PRIORITY

No matter how busy He was, Jesus spent time alone with His Father. In Mark 1:21-35 we are given a glimpse of twenty-four hours in the life of Christ. I'm out of breath just thinking about all Jesus did that day: preaching, casting out demons, traveling to the home of Simon and Andrew (while talking to James and John), healing Simon's mother-in-law, and ministering to the many who showed up on the doorstep. By sunset, I would have pulled the shades and turned out the lights. Not Jesus. He walked out the door and "cured their sick bodies and tormented spirits" (Mark 1:34).

After such a day, we wouldn't be surprised if Jesus took the next few days off, but He didn't: "Very early in the morning, while it was still dark, Jesus got up, left the house and went off to a solitary place, where he prayed" (Mark 1:35, NIV). After the busiest day in the recorded history of the life of Christ, He got up early so He could enjoy the presence of His Father. He didn't let a hectic schedule crowd out His time alone with God.

TALKING WITH HIS FATHER HELPED TO CLARIFY HIS MISSION

Jesus seemed energized by spending time alone with God. When Simon and his companions found Jesus, they said, "Everybody's looking for you!" Jesus' immediate reaction was enthusiastic: "Let's go to the rest of the villages so I can preach there also." I sense in His response a renewed passion in spite of the draining circumstances. He also came back from His time of prayer with a clear sense of His mission: "This is why I've come" (Mark 1:37-38).

Several years ago I accepted the position of director of women's ministries in my church. There were many volunteers who worked on various committees within the ministry, but I began targeting two key young women, Sarah and Nancy. I met with them and asked if they would pray about being the coordinators of the two outreach events we have for women each year. I didn't ask for an immediate commitment, but I requested that they think about this opportunity for ministry and then pray individually and together about it. Before we parted, I prayed and asked God to give them a clear picture of His vision for their immediate future.

After two weeks, they made an appointment to see me. Their radiant faces reflected their answer. Prayer had clarified their mission. Not only did they tell me yes, they told me of unchurched friends and relatives they were planning to invite. Had they committed to working on this project too quickly, they might have questioned the timing and resented the amount of work involved. However, prayer helped them focus on the aim of these events — reaching nonChristians with the gospel message — and it confirmed their personal commitment to evangelism.

TIME IN PRAYER PRODUCES RESULTS

Jesus had been making a circuit of all the towns and villages, connecting with many people. He taught in their meeting places, reported kingdom news, and healed diseased bodies and hurt lives: "When he looked out over the crowds, his heart broke. So confused and aimless they were, like sheep with no shepherd. 'What a huge harvest!' he said to his disciples. 'How few workers! On your knees and pray for harvest hands!'" (Matthew 9:36-38). He pled with the disciples to see how big the task was and how few people there were to help.

He didn't say, "You *must* get involved in this ministry! If *you* don't do it, no one else will." There was no pressure or guilt trip laid on anybody. But He passionately pled with them to get on their knees and pray for harvest hands. And the result was immediate. "The prayer was no sooner prayed than it was answered. Jesus called twelve of his followers and sent them into the ripe fields" (Matthew 10:1). As they prayed for harvest hands, some of those who were following Jesus felt God calling *them* to be the workers. They became the answer to their own prayer! Prayer always produces results. It's not always in the way we expect, but there are always results.

JESUS OFTEN WENT TO A SOLITARY PLACE TO BE ALONE WITH GOD

He often left the company of the disciples and dismissed the crowd to meet with His Father: "But Jesus often withdrew to lonely places and prayed" (Luke 5:16, NIV).

I am always amazed that Jesus seemed to find a place to pray where He was alone. As busy as our lives are, sometimes a solitary place is hard to come by — and that's where creativity comes in. Because I am frequently in my car, it has become one of my "solitary places." While I'm driving, I'm spending time alone with God. I usually begin this time by playing a CD of worship music. As I sing with the recorded music, I worship my Creator. My spirit is lifted, even in the middle of stop-and-go traffic! I converse with God about my husband — the good things and the irritating things. I talk about my concerns for our son. I tell God all my hopes and dreams as well as my disappointments and fears. I ask for wisdom about decisions, and I ask Him to continue to make me more like Jesus.

Some of you may be responding, "But Carol, I have two children under the age of five. There are *no* solitary places in my house. Being alone is impossible. Private time for prayer or Bible reading does not exist." I heard about one mother of preschoolers who let her children play on the floor in the family room while *she* got into the playpen for her time alone with God. I don't know how effective that was, but I do think it's important to plan ahead for occasional blocks of time alone with Him.

Marlae Gritter, the national director of coordinators for Moms in Touch International, encourages women to plan ahead for occasional "DAWG days" (Day Alone With God). It's a day when you schedule time with Him. It might be two hours, a full morning, or a complete day alone with God. The location might be your own home, a park, a retreat center, or the library. The structure can vary: Bible study, prayer, listening to what God says to your heart, singing or worship, reading a chapter of an inspiring biography or a book on spiritual discipline or Christian leadership. If you have young children, good friends can trade child-care responsibilities to free each other for the opportunity of enjoying God in solitude. These days can be renewing, spiritually challenging, and essential for maintaining balance.

However, don't be limited by the common definition of a "solitary place." I believe a solitary place is a state of mind that allows us to listen to God's voice in spite of outward chaos. In his book *Celebration of Discipline*, Richard Foster says:

> There is a solitude of the heart that can be maintained at all times. Crowds or the lack of them have little to do with this inward attentiveness. . . . Inward solitude will have outward manifestations. There will be the freedom to be alone, not in order to be away from people but in order to hear better. Jesus lived in inward "heart solitude." . . . We must seek out the recreating stillness of solitude if we want to be with others meaningfully.[1]

HE TAUGHT HIS DISCIPLES HOW TO PRAY

Here are just a few of Jesus' instructions:
- Don't put on airs to impress God (Matthew 6:5).
- Find a secluded place to pray (Matthew 6:6).
- Keep your prayers simple and honest (Matthew 6:7).
- Talk to God as your loving Father (Matthew 6:7-9).

- Don't follow the formulas and techniques of others (Matthew 6:7-9).
- When you fast, don't do it to impress people (Matthew 6:16-18).
- There is a time for celebration and a time for fasting (Matthew 9:14-15).

HE INFLUENCED OTHERS TO SPEND TIME WITH GOD

Jesus not only lived the seven life-changing principles covered in this book, He taught them as well. If we are to shape hearts into His image, we must do the same. If you don't feel ready or "called" to engage in a normal mentoring relationship, that's okay. Remember the results of the survey that I mentioned in chapter one? Many godly men and women had no formal mentoring relationships; instead, they were influenced by impact moments. If you desire to influence others to become like Christ, you can ask God to help you become sensitive to impact moments in which you can impart these principles. As you study these principles and seek to live them out, you will begin to influence others in life-giving ways.

So whether or not God is calling you into a formal mentoring relationship, here are some ways to impart Jesus' principle of time alone with God:

- Tell others what God is teaching you in your time with Him.
- Pray out loud together with your friend.
- Sing praise and worship songs together.
- Discuss the books and articles you are reading, and suggest reading material.

Jesus was God in the flesh; when we study Jesus, we are discovering who God is in all of His love, compassion, grace, and mercy. The more you listen, read His Word, pray, sing, and delight in Him, the more it becomes as automatic as breathing.

1. In the past twenty-four hours, when have you had time alone?

2. Read Mark 1:21-35. These verses describe twenty-four hours in the life of Christ.

    a. Make a list of every activity Jesus was involved in that day.

    b. What was His priority early the next morning?

    c. What goes through your mind when you think about getting up early to pray after a day like that?

    d. What do you think motivated Jesus to do that?

3. Read Matthew 9:36–10:1. In this situation, some of the disciples became the answer to their own prayer. Describe a time in your life when you were burdened to pray for a specific need and God asked *you* to be the one who responded to the prayer request.

4. Read Luke 5:16.

   a. Where did Jesus usually have His "quiet time"?

   b. Do you have a favorite place to spend time alone with God? If so, describe it. If not, what might your favorite place be like?

5. Describe a time in your life when you failed at doing devotions. What do you think was wrong?

6. Describe the most specific answer to a prayer request you have ever had.

7. Review the four ways that we can influence others to spend time with God (see page 28). Which ones have you used to influence someone else?

8. Read Psalm 34 aloud together. With conversational prayer, take a few minutes to express your love to Him verbally. Delight in His presence. Then ask God for anything that is on your heart. End by singing a song of praise and worship to Him!

OPTIONAL ON YOUR OWN

9. Make an appointment to interview a woman you know who has a lifetime habit of spending time alone with God. Write down questions ahead of time that will help you to make the most of your time with this person.

10. Marlae Gritter encourages women to plan ahead for "DAWG days" (Day Alone With God). What would you do if you had a whole day to concentrate on your spiritual development and personal time with God? Make a list of the activities you would most want to do on your day alone with Him, and then check your calendar. When could you schedule this opportunity? If you have young children, could you arrange to trade child-care responsibilities with a friend — perhaps another woman in your group? (Even if it can't be a whole day in the beginning, try for a morning or an afternoon.)

the principle of walking and talking

J udy Hampton recalls the influence two older women in her church had on her life:

> I didn't grow up in a Christian home. I needed mature women to teach, model, and disciple me, but never in my wildest dreams did I know it could be so much fun! Both Mary Ann and Tutty modeled the virtues of being a Christian woman. They invited me into their lives. They taught me about hospitality. I saw firsthand how they embraced their roles as wives and mothers. They gave of their time and resources. They imparted the truths from the Bible by living them in front of me (not by preaching), and put up with my endless stream of questions and desperate phone calls seeking answers. Their contagious love for Christ inspired me to seek Him every day.

If we waited for formal teaching moments to make a difference in the lives of others, most of us would miss the opportunities we have to "be Jesus" to the people we have the privilege of influencing. Whether they realized it or not, these two dear women impacted Judy's life through the principle of walking and talking.

Jesus spent three years in His public ministry walking and talking with His disciples. He didn't have the luxury of formally teaching them in a seminary classroom. They walked with Him from town to town — everywhere He went.

Whether He was teaching the disciples, visiting friends like Martha and Mary, or responding to a touch from someone in the crowd, Jesus made every contact count. The most important life lessons are almost always "caught" rather than "taught." Knowing this, Jesus took advantage of impact moments to teach and influence others, including those with whom He had chance or ordinary encounters.

How did Jesus demonstrate this principle?

JESUS TURNED INTERRUPTIONS INTO SIGNIFICANT APPOINTMENTS

One day an important man named Jairus came up to Jesus. He fell at Jesus' feet and begged Him to come to his home because his only child was dying. Jesus went with him through the pressing crowd. However, there was a woman in that crowd who had been struggling with hemorrhages for twelve years. She had already spent all of her resources on physicians who hadn't helped her condition. Working her way through the mass of people, she slipped in behind Jesus and touched the edge of his robe. The Bible says, "At that very moment her hemorrhaging stopped. Jesus said, 'Who touched me?'" (Luke 8:44-45).

Peter insisted that in a crowd of that size, dozens of people would have touched Him. But Jesus knew the difference between the press of the crowd and the touch of faith. Knowing she could no longer remain hidden, the woman knelt in front of Him, trembling. Then she told her story. Jesus said, "Daughter, you took a risk trusting me, and now you're healed and whole. Live well, live blessed!" (Luke 8:48). Afterward, Jesus went to Jairus's home and brought his daughter back to life. Jesus used this "interruption" to demonstrate that faith heals. This impact moment also taught the disciples that no person is more important to Jesus than another. The daughter of a community leader was dying, but Jesus took the time to heal a woman in the crowd.

Recently, Nan Walker answered the phone call of a marketing analyst who wanted ten minutes of her time to answer survey questions. Instead of replying that she didn't have time and hanging up, she said, "I'll answer your questions if you'll answer two of mine." The analyst agreed to her unusual request. After the survey was completed, the analyst said, "Now I'd like to hear your questions."

When Nan asked the two questions, the answers revealed that the person she was speaking to had no relationship with Jesus Christ and no hope of eternal life. So Nan asked if she could share how she came to experience personal faith in Christ and a sense of hope about the future. She explained how the woman taking the survey could have this same hope. By the end of the phone call, the analyst prayed with Nan and invited Christ into her life. By example, Nan is mentoring me in the art of turning interruptions into important appointments.

JESUS "HUNG OUT" IN PEOPLE'S HOMES

One day Jesus entered a village and went to the home of Martha and Mary. Martha made Him feel at home before she headed to the kitchen to prepare a meal. Her sister, Mary, "sat before the Master, hanging on every word he said" (Luke 10:39). Martha returned from the kitchen and interrupted Jesus and Mary. She said, "Master, don't you care that my sister has abandoned the kitchen to me? Tell her to lend me a hand" (verse 40).

Jesus said, "Martha, dear Martha, you're fussing far too much and getting yourself worked up over nothing. One thing only is essential, and Mary has chosen it — it's the main course, and won't be taken from her" (verses 41-42). Even though Jesus was relaxing in a friend's home, He made every minute count. Here He was teaching the importance of *being* over *doing*. Mary seemed to understand that who we are is more important to Jesus than what we do for Him.

As the oldest of six preacher's kids, I've always felt sorry for Martha because so many of the meal preparations for large groups of people coming to the parsonage were part of my responsibilities. I grew up feeling the urgency of "doing." For years I called my perfectionism "a pursuit of excellence."

Later I admitted to Chris, a young woman I often invited into my home, that I had been a *screaming monster*, a *silent martyr*, and a *skillful pretender* during the past because I'd been trying to impress houseguests. Behind closed doors I'd yelled at my husband, I'd been impatient with my son, and then I'd put on a big smile just in time for church (and to greet our guests) as I pretended everything was *fine*. I was fuming on the inside, while on the outside I was talking to my husband during mealtime with our guests — just enough so they wouldn't guess I was angry with him, but so he knew I was still ticked off.

I told Chris of my need to apologize to my husband and son and ask for their forgiveness for my lethal attitude and hurtful behavior. She looked at me with a shocked expression and said, "I always thought you had a *perfect* marriage and that you were an *ideal* mother. It made me think I could never be good enough to get close to you. But now, I think we could be friends." By opening my heart and home to Chris, I taught her that God was still molding me into His image. Most surprising, I learned that being vulnerable about my sins and weaknesses made me a more desirable person to get to know.

JESUS TOOK HIS DISCIPLES WITH HIM WHEN HE TRAVELED AND PREACHED

"Jesus made a circuit of all the towns and villages. He taught in their meeting places, reported kingdom news, and healed their diseased bodies, healed their bruised and hurt lives" (Matthew 9:35). Every day for three years Jesus allowed His followers to accompany Him while He traveled, preached, healed, told stories, taught object lessons, and gave instruction. In this way, His disciples were able to see that He both "walked and talked" His message.

If we want to impact others for Christ, we will invite women to accompany us when we teach a Bible study or go to a retreat. It's important to let women get close enough to see how we juggle our ministry lives and our personal lives. Perhaps we'll invite them to go grocery shopping, or to a concert with us, or to join our family at the zoo for a day. Married or single, we can invite women to our homes so they can feel invited into our lives and observe how we interact with our spouses and children or roommates. They will learn as much by what they observe in our interaction with our families and coworkers as they do from our carefully prepared instruction.

Jesus' "Walk and Talk" Was a Powerful Witnessing Tool

Jesus seized every opportunity to talk about the kingdom of God, even if the hearer wasn't ready to accept the whole story right away (John 3:1-18 is a good example). We can do the same thing.

Deborah Henry left her job at an investment research firm. She was tired of working for an authoritarian boss who barked commands at her and didn't have "please" and "thank you" in his vocabulary. When she took a new job as assistant to a prolific Christian author, she expected the same brash treatment. After all, he was a *man* with power and authority over her!

However, during her first year as his assistant, she noticed a gentleness in his tone of voice, even when he was under enormous pressure. He was firm but didn't repay injury with injury. He seemed unconcerned about taking credit, yet gave it freely to people who needed it — including her!

Unlike her previous employer, he treated her as kindly as he treated his highly impressive professional friends and associates. He valued her comments and complimented her work. She began to feel purposeful and significant.

Deborah became curious about the way he handled his life,

compared with the way she handled her own life. Working with this man was like breathing fresh air for the first time, and she sensed from his marriage, his work relationships, and his children that life could be different. She states, "He was the first man who treated me with unconditional respect, not because I deserved his respect, but because he treated everyone he met with respect. The doorman in the elevator received the same smile that the president of the United States did."

Deborah's curiosity grew as her boss instilled in her a sense of worth that made her willing to dare to search for deeper meaning in her obscure existence. One day he asked for her opinion about a line in a book he was writing. "What do you think of this line?" he asked. The line described the main character's search for the meaning of life.

Deborah immediately said, "I think it should say he was trying to find his *center*."

"I like that." he said. "That's very good . . . finding one's center. Very nicely put."

As Deborah looked at her kind employer, she knew that he understood what it meant to be *centered*. She visualized her own center as a deep, dark well. She blurted out, "I yearn for wholeness, too. . . . Something big is missing. I've been going to church on my lunch break . . . looking for a home. Do you go to church?"

That day a busy man took the time to share his faith with Deborah, a struggling employee who was hungry for God. Soon after this meaningful conversation, Deborah found her *center* in Jesus Christ.

Deborah's employer demonstrated such Christlike characteristics through his daily "walking and talking" that she longed for a personal relationship with the Savior. Like Christ, this man's daily lifestyle was his strongest witnessing tool.

JESUS WALKED WHAT HE TALKED, AND TALKED WHAT HE WALKED

Jesus both lived what He believed and talked openly about what He believed. Here's what He said about keeping our walk (behavior) and talk congruent.

Be salt-seasoning. "Let me tell you why you are here. You're here to be salt-seasoning that brings out the God-flavors of this earth. If you lose your saltiness, how will people taste godliness? You've lost your usefulness and will end up in the garbage" (Matthew 5:13). Salt enhances flavor and also acts as a preservative. We become salt through bringing the essence of Jesus into everyday conversation. We influence others by being Christ to them.

Go public with your faith. Jesus said, "You're here to be light, bringing out the God-colors in the world. God is not a secret to be kept. We're going public with this, as public as a city on a hill. If I make you light-bearers, you don't think I'm going to hide you under a bucket, do you? I'm putting you on a light stand. Now that I've put you there on a hilltop, on a light stand — shine!" (Matthew 5:14-16).

Let people "hang out" with you. Jesus taught, "Keep open house; be generous with your lives. By opening up to others, you'll prompt people to open up with God, this generous Father in heaven" (Matthew 5:16).

Barb McPhail says, "When I welcomed Christ into my life as Lord and Savior, I was a twenty-four-year-old party girl." She explains, "My prayer of repentance was, 'Goodbye Schuberg's Bar. Goodbye party buddies. Hello Jesus!'" She found herself longing for a friend and mentor who would help her get to know Christ better. Within a few months God replaced her former party friends with the love and support of a thirty-three-year-old wife and mother who loved God. She said,

In the sixteen years since we met, Lee has been my mother, sister, best friend, prayer part-ner, and adviser. Like an empty sponge, I eagerly soaked up all the love and insight about

God's kingdom she had to offer. She never professed to have all the answers, but she was quick to say, "Let's pray." To this day, whenever I hear those words, I'm reminded that God fulfilled the desire of my heart for a friend and mentor through Lee.

When we allow a younger woman to spend time with us daily (not just during special appointments, Bible studies, and lunch dates), we give her a chance to see how a Christian should live her life. She may at times see examples of when we blow it with our husbands, roommates, children, or friends, but it's an honest view of life.

Accentuate your strengths and minimize your liabilities. Too many women feel they can't be a positive influence if they have not "arrived" spir-.itually. But the best mentor is one who admits failure and allows a younger woman to watch her deal with the effects of failure (or sin) and learn from the process. The only perfect mentor who ever lived was Jesus. If you are waiting for that level of perfection before you make yourself available, it won't happen.

Continue to grow spiritually yourself. The best mentor is someone who walks and talks with Jesus every day. Your Christian life becomes a natural rhythm of assimilating God's Word into your heart and life and translating what you learn into practical daily living.

It's never easy to add an "unpaid" job to your life. It means the sacrifice of time. However, a woman with Christ's heart says, "God has taught me so much, and my greatest joy would be to help someone avoid some of the mistakes I made and to give her encouragement when life gets hard."

1. If a younger believer had spent time with you during the past twenty-four hours, what could she have learned about the life of a Christian?

2. Jesus often took advantage of "impact moments" to teach and influence as He encountered people during the activities of an average day.

    a.   Read Luke 8:40-55. How did Jesus turn an interruption into an impact moment?

    b.   Read Luke 10:38-42. How did Jesus turn this visit into an opportunity to teach and influence others?

3. This chapter contains several stories of women who went out of their way to influence others as Jesus did. Which story touches you the most, and why?

- Tutty and Mary Ann, who influenced Judy Hampton

- Nan Walker, who influenced the marketing analyst

- the author (Carol Kent), who influenced Chris

- Lee, who influenced Barb McPhail

4. Jesus took His disciples with Him when He traveled and preached. They learned much by watching the way He interacted with people as He healed, told stories, taught object lessons, and gave instruction.

   Think of a woman who modeled Christlike behavior and taught you practical Christian truth by the way she lived. What specific things did you learn from her example?

5. Have you ever had an opportunity to influence someone else at an unexpected moment? If so, describe that experience.

6. Reread the story of Deborah Henry on pages 39-40.

   a. What made her employer's daily treatment of her such a powerful, evangelistic tool?

b. In what situations do you have the opportunity to extend kindness and respect to unbelievers? (Think, for example, of coworkers, your children's friends, the parents of those friends, people with whom you share a hobby, and so on.)

7. Read Matthew 5:13 (MSG). What do you think the Bible means by "salt-seasoning"? Give some examples that you might encounter in a typical week.

8. Think back over the past week. Can you recall any instances when you could have influenced another person positively? For example,

• When could you have hung around with a younger believer and encouraged her faith?

- When could you have taken a younger believer along with you as you did ministry or just lived life?

- When could you have demonstrated your faith by the way you lived at work or at school?

9. What's your reaction to the idea that you don't have to have "arrived" spiritually to be a valuable influence in someone's life?

10. What would it cost you to invite a younger believer to hang out with you? What are the potential benefits?

11. Share with the group your deepest hope or fear about influencing others as Jesus did. How can the group pray for you this week? Take time to pray for these requests.

chapter four

the principle of asking questions

early in our marriage, when Gene and I were youth directors in our church, one sixteen-year-old named Char seemed bent on a path of destruction. She verbally put herself down. She got into alcohol and drug abuse, and she hung out with other teens who were making negative choices. With her mouth she told us that she wanted to live for God and make decisions that reflected a Christian lifestyle, but her behavior reflected another story.

I invited Char to our home while Gene was away, and during a relaxing, nonthreatening visit, I asked her the following questions:

- *"Are the choices you are making right now making you happy?"* That was a given; she definitely wasn't happy.
- *"What benefits are you receiving from your current lifestyle?"* I urged her to be open about this, and her answers were truthful — friends, acceptance, instant gratification, and so on.
- *"What do you want your life to be like five years from now?"* To a teenager, that's an eternity, but it did make her think about where her current choices might lead.
- *"Char, which do you love more: Jesus, or what you are doing to destroy your body and mind? It's your choice."* I had wept with her and prayed with her. Our relationship was close enough for me to be this confrontational. She cried with me as she answered that question.
- *"What can I do to help you? You've said you love Jesus more than your addiction to drugs and alcohol. Are you willing to follow through with getting professional help for these addictions? Could I be an accountability partner in your life?"*

My questions — combined with listening, love, and God's intervention — helped Char to see what dangerous ground she had been walking on. The next few months proved to be a difficult struggle for Char, but she made better choices and began to change her behavior.

Who would have thought that a question could be so powerful? And yet, that is often the case. According to authors Robert and Pamela Crosby, "Good questions create interest; great ones inspire a response. Good questions open conversations; great ones open souls. Good questions raise issues; great ones evoke dreams and visions. Good questions elicit ideas; great questions uncover needs."[1]

Jesus asked questions that opened people's souls, uncovering long-held dreams and deep-seated needs. Sometimes He used questions to bring conviction or reveal hypocrisy. His questions often made people think about who He was and why He came. Let's take a closer look at the ways in which He used questions.

JESUS USED QUESTIONS TO EXPOSE FALSEHOOD AND REVEAL TRUTH

At times Jesus asked questions to reveal what was truly in people's hearts. For example, the Pharisees represented themselves as people who loved and obeyed God, but in reality, they were hypocrites.

Jesus entered the temple courts, and, while he was teaching, the chief priests and the elders of the people came to him. "By what authority are you doing these things?" they asked. "And who gave you this authority?"

Jesus replied, "I will also ask you one question. If you answer me, I will tell you by what authority I am doing these things. John's baptism — where did it come from? Was it from heaven, or of human origin?"

They discussed it among themselves and said, "If we say, 'From heaven,' he will ask, 'Then why didn't you believe him?' But if we say, 'of human origin' — we are afraid of the *people, for they all hold that John was a prophet."*

So they answered Jesus, "We don't know."

Then he said, "Neither will I tell you by what authority I am doing these things."
(Matthew 21:23-27, NIV)

Jesus knew that the Pharisees weren't sincere when they asked Him by whose authority He performed miracles; He knew they wanted to accuse Him of blasphemy and were trying to trick Him. So He answered their question with another question, exposing what was really in their hearts.

Women of influence often have people who come to them for help. Many times the plea is sincere, but not always. Sometimes it is wise for us to ask questions that will expose whether or not the person truly wants 100 percent spiritual healing or whether she enjoys being needy.

JESUS' QUESTIONS EXPOSED PEOPLE'S DEEPEST LONGINGS

One day a blind beggar heard that Jesus was passing by. He cried out, "Jesus, son of David, have mercy on me!" Jesus stopped and asked the man to be brought to Him. His first words were a question: "What do you want me to do for you?" The man replied, "Lord, I want to see" (Luke 18:41, NIV).

What do you want me to do for you? When you are approached by a woman who wants to spend time with you, ask her this question. Does she want advice, a listening ear, to be discipled, a friend? Her answer can direct you in how you spend your time together, and it can give you important information about how insightful and self-aware she might be. Some of the questions I ask women to help them realize their deepest longings are:

• What are the five most important things in your life?

- What stress point are you experiencing that you would like to eliminate?

- What one thing would you like to change about your body?

- What one thing would you like to see change in your spiritual life?

- What were your expectations when you got married?

- What were your expectations when you had your first baby?

- In what area of your life do you need advice?

- What woman (historical or contemporary) would you most like to emulate?

- What did you want to grow up to do or to be? Have you fulfilled that dream?

Every time I ask one of these questions and the woman answers it honestly, we're drawn closer together. I try never to act shocked with the responses — even if I am. When longings are discussed, it's important to provide a safe place for honest answers.

JESUS' QUESTIONS TRIGGERED GROWTH IN FAITH

In an article titled "The Questions of Jesus," Todd Catteau comments:

> *Jesus . . . asked faith-building questions after episodes that demonstrated a lack of faith. In Matthew 14:31, for example, Jesus rescued Peter from his failed attempt to walk on water, then asked, "Why did you doubt?" That question had to ring in Peter's ears for the rest of his life and probably helped him through many other challenging situations.*[2]

You and I can do the same when working with people whose faith is going through tough times. During my assignment as director of the alternative education program for pregnant teenagers, Tammy entered my life. She was a dynamic, attractive, energized high school senior and captain of the cheerleading squad until she got pregnant. She and Brad, the star quarterback of the football team, were in love, but they were both seventeen and decided to wait to get married.

Tammy went from being one of the most popular girls in the senior class to leaving her school because of the pregnancy and coming to alternative ed to finish her classes so she could graduate. She was "pretty sure" of Brad's love, but she had seen him flirt with other girls and her confidence in their relationship was deteriorating.

One day Tammy blurted out, "I've wrecked my life. I've hurt my parents. I used to be pretty, but now I'm big and fat. I don't know if I can trust Brad to stay true to me. I'm just so afraid."

Putting my arm around her, I asked, "Tammy, what are you afraid of?" She was most fearful of not having a husband and being a single mother with no future. I said, "Tammy, you told me you became a Christian just two years ago. Do you believe God will give you the strength to bring this baby into the world and to be a good mother — even if Brad isn't in your life?"

"Y-y-yes," she said.

I continued, "Do you know there's a verse in the Bible that says, 'Never will I leave you; never will I forsake you'?³ What that really means is that God says He will never let you down and never walk off and leave you. The next verse says, 'The Lord is my helper; I will not be afraid. . . .' Do you believe God will take care of you, Tammy?"

She wiped her tears and meekly, but honestly, said, "Yes, but right now I'd rather have Brad." We both laughed, but I saw a new confidence in her eyes.

THE MOST IMPORTANT QUESTION JESUS ASKED

As Jesus and the disciples were heading out for the villages around Caesarea Philippi, He asked them, "Who do the people say I am?" (Mark 8:27).

The disciples responded that some people thought He was John the Baptist and others thought He was Elijah, and still others thought He was one of the prophets. Jesus then asked them, "And you — what are you saying about me? Who am I?" (verse 29).

Peter gave the answer. "You are the Christ, the Messiah" (verse 29).

Probably the most important question Jesus ever asked was, "Who am I?" If the disciples got the right answer to *that* question, they understood His purpose for coming and they would understand their mission when He was gone. As we invest time in people, we need to be sure they understand *who Jesus is*. If they believe He was a great teacher, an extraordinary humanitarian, and a compassionate person, they have not yet come to know Him personally. Once they can acknowledge, as Peter did, "He is Christ, the Messiah — *my* Messiah," they are on their way to a personal relationship with God.

JESUS KNEW HIS AUDIENCE

Jesus seemed to "read" His audience and then form a question that was perfect for that person. He had a *confrontational* question for the Pharisee: Did John's baptism come from heaven or men?; a *tender* question for the woman taken in adultery: Where are your accusers?; and a *revealing* question for the disciples: Who do you say that I am?

As we begin mentoring younger women, we need to know our "audience." And getting to know a woman God has put in your life is one of the great joys of the journey. Here are some questions I use when I'm getting to know a woman I am mentoring:

- What were your growing-up years like?
- What is your best memory of your father? Your mother?
- What is your favorite old movie?
- What kind of music do you like?
- How did your family celebrate Christmas?
- In what part of your life do you feel vulnerable?
- What one thing would you like to do before you die?
- What keeps you from being as close to the Lord as you'd like to be?

The most important question you can ask someone is, *How did you come to know Christ?* Her enthusiasm — or lack of it — will tell you whether or not she is passionate about her walk with the Lord.

JESUS ASKED QUESTIONS THAT COULDN'T BE ANSWERED WITH A "YES" OR A "NO"

The best coaches and teachers learn how to ask questions that require more than a quick, trite answer. Here are some questions that can't be answered with a "yes" or "no":

- What are your strengths? Your weaknesses?

- If you had a completely free day, what would you do?

- What are your hobbies, interests, and passions?

- If money were not an issue, what would you do with the rest of your life?

- What's the biggest roadblock between you and your dream?

- What would you change about yourself if you had the chance?

- If you could interview any historical person, who would it be and what would you ask?

- In what two specific areas would you like to see yourself grow during the next one to three years?

- What is the biggest answer to prayer you've ever experienced?

- What is your favorite Scripture verse and why does it mean so much to you?

- What do you like best about your job? Least?

- What does the Scripture say about this?

- How can I pray for you?

A chapter about the principle of asking questions should definitely end with a question. As you come to grips with the love Christ has for you, will you consider becoming a person who influences the lives of others *intentionally*? Who will *you* tell that Jesus Christ has transformed your life?

1. Let each woman in the group choose one of the getting-to-know-you questions on page 56 and answer it. After all have answered a question, talk about which questions seemed to be the most helpful in deepening your knowledge of each other.

2. Read Luke 18:35-43. Jesus asked, "What do you want me to do for you?" Why do you think He asked a question that seemed to have such an obvious answer?

3. Read Mark 8:27-30.

    a. Why do you think Jesus' question to Peter, "Who do you say I am?" was so important?

    b. If Jesus asked you today, "Who do you say I am?" how would you respond?

4. Carefully read Matthew 21:23-27.

    a. What was the question the chief priests and the elders asked Jesus?

b. Why do you think Jesus didn't answer their question?

5. Review the story of Char on pages 49-50. Why do you think a series of questions sometimes gets through to a person's heart more effectively than a lecture?

6. Let each group member choose one of the questions about deepest longings (page 51-53) and answer it. Have someone jot notes. When everyone has responded, use these as the basis for a time of praying for each other.

OPTIONAL ON YOUR OWN

7. One of the best ways to get to know a friend or someone you are mentoring is to ask good questions. During the next week, invite a younger woman (or a friend) over for coffee and ask the following questions. It might help you to be better prepared if you write out your own answers to these questions before you ask someone else to respond.

• What are your strengths? Your weaknesses?

- If you had a completely free day, what would you do?

- If money were not an issue, what would you do with the rest of your life?

- What is the biggest roadblock between you and your dream?

- In what two specific areas would you like to see yourself grow during the next one to three years?

- What is the biggest answer to prayer you've ever experienced?

- What is your favorite Scripture verse and why does it mean so much to you?

- What would you like to do for God in your lifetime?

- How can I help you?

- How can I pray for you?

chapter five

the principle of compassion

Ruth Winslow works in China as a health care professional and vocational counselor, primarily with people who have been cured of leprosy. Even though these people no longer have the disease, they are still marked and considered "detestable" because the drug that cures leprosy also leaves a huge scar on their faces and limbs. Many are still forced to live as outcasts in government-designated areas of mainland China.

Ruth's heart broke as she visited these outcasts. Even though they have received physical healing, many are not able to get jobs or make a decent wage. Most have few possessions and suffer greatly from the emotional pain of being shunned by society. But God called Ruth to help these dear people in a very practical and tangible way — she determined to equip them with the skill and means to earn an income.

After hours and hours of paperwork and red tape, Ruth arranged for sewing machines to be brought into one of these villages. Once the machines arrived, Ruth taught the adults how to make quilts for babies. With the help of numerous mission organizations, many of these quilts are being marketed and sold in the United States. Ruth's face lights up as she speaks of the hope and sense of purpose that this task has nurtured in these people.

One day she was cleaning the ulcerated feet of one of the men in the village. He'd had leprosy for years and his feet were extremely disfigured. To have his feet touched, let alone cleaned, by someone who had never had the disease must have been an unusual experience. Looking up, her eyes met his and he whispered, "Thank you."

Ruth's instant response was, "Thank Jesus."

He paused, looked her in the eyes again, and said, "*You* are Jesus."

Jesus told His disciples, "What a huge harvest!... How few workers! On your knees and pray for harvest hands!" (Matthew 9:37). Ruth is one of those "harvest hands." Through her ministry in leper colonies, she demonstrates compassion. Not only was her heart saddened by the plight of these people, she did something about it. Like Jesus, she was not afraid to touch people who have long been considered untouchable.

If we want to influence lives as Jesus did, we, too, must have a compassionate heart. Compassion is the heart's response to a person's need combined with a helping hand that offers mercy and grace. The word *compassion* means "to have pity (and) a feeling of distress from the ills of others, to suffer with another... to alleviate the consequences of sin or suffering in the lives of others... to moderate one's anger (and) treat with mildness, moderation, and gentleness."[1]

Before we can communicate compassion, we must see another's woundedness and be saddened by it.

JESUS NOTICED PEOPLE'S NEEDS

Over and over, the Gospels tell how Jesus' heart broke with compassion for people.

"Then Jesus made a circuit of all the towns and villages. He taught in their meeting places, reported kingdom news, and healed their diseased bodies, healed their bruised and hurt lives. When he looked out over the crowds, his heart broke. So confused and aimless they were, like sheep with no shepherd." (Matthew 9:35-36)

The text says, "When he *looked out* over the crowds." The passage doesn't tell us how Jesus felt, but we can imagine that He had been walking for miles and miles. He must have been exhausted after days of teaching and healing people, but instead of getting irritated or feeling hassled, Jesus *noticed* the people's confusion and neediness. He *noticed* people who needed healing, both spiritually and physically.

When the Pharisees criticized Him for spending so much time with the outcasts of the day — tax collectors and sinners — Jesus replied, "It is not the healthy who need a doctor, but the sick" (Matthew 9:12, NIV). Jesus sought out people who needed compassion. They were the very people He came to heal and save.

How different that is from most of us! On the way home from a retreat recently, I lugged my carry-ons to my assigned seat on the aircraft, shoved my garment bag into the overhead compartment, and fell into my seat. As I was putting my briefcase underneath the seat in front of me, I caught a side glance of the woman next to me. She had graying hair and was nervously clutching her purse. I figured she hadn't flown much. By the look on her face, I knew opening a conversation could mean a nonstop chat.

Exhausted after speaking at a three-day conference, I had looked forward to a nap on the plane before my ninety-minute drive home from the airport. I smiled and nodded in her direction, and then buckled my seat belt and closed my eyes, indicating I intended to sleep.

My plan worked. I had my nap and avoided a conversation. Much later, the pilot's voice came over the loudspeaker, announcing our descent. Opening my eyes, I glanced in the woman's direction. As soon as we made eye contact, she said, "I just buried my sister yesterday."

"Oh, I'm so sorry to hear about your loss," I said.

She continued, "We buried our mother a year ago this week. There's not much to live for anymore."

At that moment the wheels of the plane hit the runway, and I knew our flight was almost over. My words of hope were delivered too late and too rushed. The two of us gathered up our belongings and parted, still strangers.

I don't know if this woman knew Jesus or not because I didn't take the time to speak with her earlier in the trip. She had wanted to talk. I wanted to sleep. And because I failed to see people as Jesus saw people, I lost an opportunity to touch this woman's heart with Jesus' love and compassion.

TOUCH CAN COMMUNICATE COMPASSION

Jesus demonstrated that having a compassionate heart often includes a healing touch:

> Jesus came down the mountain with the cheers of the crowd still ringing in his ears. Then a leper appeared and went to his knees before Jesus, praying, "Master, if you want to, you can heal my body."
>
> Jesus reached out and touched him, saying, "I want to. Be clean." Then and there, all signs of the leprosy were gone. Jesus said, "Don't talk about this all over town. Just quietly present your healed body to the priest, along with the appropriate expressions of thanks to God. Your cleansed and grateful life, not your words, will bear witness to what I have done." (Matthew 8:1-4)

Jesus' touch was not what healed the man. His *word* wiped out the disease. But His touch — before the word that brought healing — was pure compassion. Jesus' compassionate touch validated the man's worth, affirmed his personhood, and revived his hope. You and I may not have the same ability to heal people as Jesus did, but we can offer a "healing touch," whether through a warm hug, a simple squeeze of an arm, a gentle touch on a shoulder, or a lingering handshake.

A REFLECTION OF THE FATHER'S HEART

Jesus told many stories that reflect the heart of a compassionate Father, but none better than the story of a father who had two sons. The younger son wanted his inheritance immediately. The father divided the property between the two sons, and the undisciplined son left and wasted everything he had. Finally, reduced to slopping pigs, he realized his father's farmhands had a better life than he had.

He came home to tell his father he didn't deserve to be his son and that he wanted to work for him as a hired hand. "But while he was still a long way off, his father saw him and was filled with compassion for him; he ran to his son, threw his arms around him and kissed him" (Luke 15:20, NIV). The son confessed his sin, but the father wasn't listening. He was so excited and happy that his son had returned, he was already making plans for a celebration.

When the older son came in from the fields and learned that his father had ordered a feast in honor of his wayward brother's safe return home, he was so angry he stalked off and refused to join in. His father tried to talk to him, but he wouldn't listen. The son said, "Look how many years I've stayed here serving you, never giving you one moment of grief, but have you ever thrown a party for me and my friends? Then this son of yours who has thrown away your money on whores shows up and you go all out with a feast!"

His father said, "Son, you don't understand. You're with me all the time, and everything that is mine is yours — but this is a wonderful time, and we had to celebrate. This brother of yours was dead, and he's alive! He was lost, and he's found!" (verses 28-32).

When I first heard this story, I empathized with the older son — perhaps because as a teen, I never rebelled or caused my parents grief. I felt it was unfair that the brother who squandered his inheritance received such royal treatment. Why would the father throw such a huge party for a son who had disappointed him so severely?

Today, however, I realize this story defines true compassion. The father of the prodigal son loved both sons equally, but he showed compassion to the one who needed it. We don't show compassion because someone in our life deserves it, earns it, or works for it. And if our hearts reflect harshness, unforgiveness, criticism, judgment, hardness, or enmity — especially to those who have repented — we are not treating people as Jesus did. We may still influence them — but not in a way that edifies them or brings God glory!

How Can You and I Show Compassion?

Jess Moody offers insight about how to show compassion:

> Did you ever take a real trip down inside the broken heart of a friend? To feel the sob of the soul — the raw, red crucible of emotional agony? To have this become almost as much yours as that of your soulcrushed neighbor? Then, to sit down with him — and silently weep? This is the beginning of compassion.[2]

If we are going to become women of compassion, we need to do the following:
- See a woman's need.
- Feel her pain (or need).
- Get involved (instead of walking by or passing the buck).
- Weep with her (show empathy).
- Extend support and help — hands-on, if possible. (Remember, Jesus *touched* people wherever He went.)
- Wait with the woman (in spirit or in person) until her needy situation is resolved.

Ideas for Practicing Compassion

Here are some ideas about how you can show more compassion to someone you are mentoring. (Or consider inviting her to join you in giving one of these compassionate gifts to someone else who needs encouragement.)
- If she has young children, offer to baby-sit so she can have a few peaceful hours alone or go shopping with a friend.
- Cook a meal for her family or household on her busiest day of the

week. If possible, deliver the meal, serve it, and stay to clean up the mess.

- Purchase two registrations for a women's conference and surprise someone with an unexpected inspirational weekend away from home. Help her to arrange for child-care if she has small children.
- Find out about any days that trigger sadness in the lives of those you are mentoring — the anniversary of the death of a child, parent, or spouse. Send flowers or a card to let the person know you are covering her with prayer on this particular day.
- If possible, take her to lunch and ask questions that give her an opportunity to talk about a departed loved one.
- Invite her to go with you when you take a mentally or physically challenged person to the store or to an appointment.
- If her funds are limited, place a sack of groceries on her doorstep, ring the doorbell, and leave. Have a note inside the grocery sack that says, "From someone who loves you and hopes you enjoy every bite."
- Invite her to accompany you on a visit to a convalescent home. If she has musical gifts, encourage her to sing to some of the patients. Take turns reading short inspirational or humorous stories to individual patients.
- Ask her, "What's the toughest situation you've had to deal with this week?"
- Listen carefully as she answers, and give her a safe place to vent frustrations, fears, and concerns. Offer genuine compassion and biblical counsel, then take the time to pray with her about what she's struggling with.

Remember, compassion is not simply feeling sad about someone's pain or circumstances, it is also *doing something* to alleviate the pain. If you're ready for an adventure, try doing three intentional acts of compassion this week — and watch how God works in your heart as well as in the hearts of those lives you touch!

1. When have you experienced compassion from someone else?

2. Read Matthew 14:13-14. This passage explains what Jesus did right after He got the news that John the Baptist, His cousin and forerunner, had been beheaded.

   a. What was Jesus trying to do?

   b. How was He interrupted?

   c. What was His response?

d. If you were Jesus' friend, and a key person in His life had just been killed, what would you have thought about His response to this situation?

3. Read Luke 15:11-31.

a. What phrases in this passage show the father's compassion?

b. How does this story demonstrate Jesus' model of compassion?

c. How does the response of the older brother demonstrate the opposite of compassion?

4. Review the story of Ruth Winslow's work in China on pages 65-66. How does Ruth demonstrate "being Jesus" to the people she works with?

5. What are some of the specific needs you see in the lives of the women in your immediate sphere of influence?

6. On a scale of 1 to 10, how would you rate your "compassion quotient"?

(Lowest)   (Highest)
    1   2   3   4   5   6   7   8   9   10

7. Corrie ten Boom once said, "What have you done today that only a Christian would have done?"[3] Review the six bulleted points on page 70 that remind us of the steps involved in showing compassion. Which step is the one you most need to grow in right now?

8. How can the group pray for you this week? Take some time to pray for each other's needs. Whether you are more like the younger brother or the older brother in the Luke 15 story, thank your Father for His compassion toward you.

OPTIONAL ON YOUR OWN

9. Using the suggestions in this chapter as a guideline, take a practical step of compassion toward another person this week.

chapter six

the principle of unconditional love

No one has ever loved us more completely or undeservedly than Jesus. When He lived on this earth, He didn't love some people and not others. He didn't love people because of how they treated Him or because of what they thought of Him. He loved everyone equally and unequivocally. Some people were surprised by His love, and others never even recognized it. Certainly, none of us deserves His love. Just ask the Samaritan woman.

One day, on His way to Galilee, Jesus passed through Samaria. He came to a Samaritan village and, exhausted, sat down by the village well. A Samaritan woman came to draw water. Jesus said to her, "Would you give me a drink of water?" (John 4:7). She was taken aback. Why was a Jew asking a Samaritan woman for a drink?

Jesus launched a conversation about "living water," water that would take away the woman's thirst *forever*. Intrigued, she asked Him for this water. He told her to call her husband and then come back. She said she had no husband. Jesus replied that her words were true — she'd had five husbands, and the man she was living with wasn't her spouse.

On this, *The Quest Study Bible* comments: "Divorce in the Jewish-Samaritan culture could only be initiated by the husband, who had to state publicly that his wife was unclean, unlovable, or incapable of fulfilling her wifely duties. Divorce therefore shamed a woman. And now she was most likely living with her current partner simply to avoid starvation."[1]

THE NEGATIVE IMPACT OF "CONDITIONAL LOVE"

What had happened to this woman's sense of significance when society announced that she was an unclean, undesirable woman — *five times?* I meet many women who have endured similar rejection, and their wounds are deep. Can you feel the pain beneath the following words?

- "I'm single and never feel like my parents love me as much as my siblings who married and produced grandchildren for them. They treat me as if I'm incomplete without a husband. I'm sick of hearing them ask, 'Are there any new men in your life?'"
- "My mother-in-law has never accepted me and loved me as her daughter because I didn't come from the right social background to be worthy of her son. She will never know the joy she's missed by rejecting me."
- "I was a promiscuous woman for many years before I met Jesus, and people in my church can't seem to forget the woman I used to be and accept me as the forgiven woman I am today."

Each of these women was hurt by someone whose love was conditional. Most of us, at some time or another, have endured rejection, unforgiveness, or unloving responses from people we longed to have love us. Most of us have experienced the feeling of being unlovable in at least one area of our lives. Our unspoken cry is *Please love me!* When you and I listen to people's stories without judging them, we are taking the first step in practicing unconditional love.

Jesus talked to the woman at the well about the racial and religious prejudices that separated the Jews and the Samaritans. How healing His words must have been!

The time is coming — it has, in fact, come — when what you're called will not matter and where you go to worship will not matter. It's who you are and the way you live that count

before God. Your worship must engage your spirit in the pursuit of truth. That's the kind
of people the Father is out looking for: those who are simply and honestly themselves
before him in their worship. (John 4:23)

Just as Jesus was identifying Himself as the Messiah, His disciples arrived. They were shocked that Jesus was talking with *that kind* of a woman. "No one said what they were all thinking, but their faces showed it" (verse 27). The woman took the hint and left in such a hurry she forgot her water pot. But when she got to the village, she told the people, "'Come see a man who knew all about the things I did, who knows me inside and out. Do you think this could be the Messiah?' And they went out to see for themselves" (verse 29).

Jesus loved this woman unconditionally — and because He did, she had a new confidence. Her immediate response was to tell people about the man who knew her "inside and out." She planted seeds of faith in the hearts of all she spoke to.

THE THREE STAGES OF LOVING OTHERS

We cannot practice the principle of unconditional love apart from practicing the principle of compassion. Compassion and unconditional love go hand in hand.

John Powell writes,

In the process of loving there are three important stages or moments:

  1. Kindness: a warm assurance that "I am on your side. I care about you."

  2. Encouragement: a strong reassurance of your own strength. . . .

  3. Challenge: a loving but firm exhortation to action. . . . The first thing love must do
is communicate these three things: I truly care about you. I really want your happiness, and
I will do all I can to assure it. You are a uniquely valuable person.[2]

Jesus' treatment of the Samaritan woman illustrates this definition. It was *kind* for Jesus — a Jew — to engage a Samaritan woman in conversation. Jews had only disdain for Samaritans, whom they saw as inferior. Jesus' behavior told her she was valuable. He *encouraged* her by affirming her truthfulness about the fact that she had no husband. And by the end of their conversation, He had *challenged* her to discover that He was indeed the Messiah.

Unconditional love is not concerned about what someone *did;* it does not use *appearance* as a measuring stick for personal worth. Nor does unconditional love throw the past into the face of someone who hasn't asked for our forgiveness, even if he or she has wronged us. In fact, Jesus said, "I'm telling you to love your enemies. Let them bring out the best in you, not the worst. . . . If all you do is love the lovable, do you expect a bonus? Anybody can do that. . . . In a word, what I'm saying is, *Grow up.* You're kingdom subjects. Now live like it" (Matthew 5:44,46,48).

JESUS DEMONSTRATED HIS TEACHINGS ON LOVE

Jesus also said, "This is my command: Love one another the way I loved you. This is the very best way to love. Put your life on the line for your friends" (John 15:12-13). Giving your life out of love for someone else is the highest demonstration of unconditional love.

> *This is how much God loved the world: He gave his Son, his one and only Son. And this is why: so that no one need be destroyed; by believing in him, anyone can have a whole and lasting life. God didn't go to all the trouble of sending his Son merely to point an accusing finger, telling the world how bad it was. He came to help, to put the world right again.*
> *(John 3:16-17)*

Jesus was God, yet He humbled Himself to become one cell in a woman's womb. He grew to maturity, went into public ministry, and men that He created yelled, "You're not the man you claim to be!" Religious leaders accused Him of blasphemy and schemed to get rid of Him. One of His own disciples betrayed Him. He was tortured and mocked. Finally, He faced a death so horrible it was usually reserved for foreigners and slaves.

The sinless Son of God could have said, "No, I will not go through this pain." But He didn't. God proved His love on the cross. When Christ hung, and bled, and died, it was God saying to the world, "I love you."[3] That's unconditional love. We never deserved it. We couldn't do enough to earn it. We simply receive it.

If you're reading this book and for the first time you realize how much God loves you — personally — and you desire to begin a walk of faith with Him, pause for a moment. Bow your head and pray, "Lord, I acknowledge that I need You in my life. I'm tired of trying to pick myself up by my own ability. I need Your forgiveness, and I realize when Jesus died on the cross it was because He loved me *unconditionally* and paid the price for my wrongdoing. I know He did not stay dead — He rose from the grave. I confess my sin and invite Jesus to be my Savior. Come into my life and help me to live for You. In Jesus' name. Amen."

If you just prayed that prayer, you have received the unconditional love and forgiveness of God and you are part of a new family — God's family.

LOVING OTHERS AS JESUS DID

How, then, can you and I practice this principle and ignite it in others?

I believe that it is a mark of spiritual maturity when Christians have a few people of "doubtful reputation" within our circle of friends. The words "doubtful reputation" may sound a bit severe, but I think we need to ask women we mentor to occasionally spend time with us when we are with nonChristians who may have a drastically different lifestyle than they are used to.

During my early years of teaching, I developed a friendship with another teacher who had been "dumped" by her husband so he could go back to partying like a single guy. Whenever I visited her, she always played Carly Simon's song, "You're So Vain." She said she played this song over and over because it reminded her of the selfish, uncaring, egocentric, self-indulgent clod of a man she had once been married to. Lori needed the Lord if she was ever going to become free from the anger and hopelessness of her situation.

One afternoon I invited Sarah, a young woman I was mentoring, to come over for coffee to meet Lori. Sarah was from a conservative Christian home and had been married for only a short time.

As soon as Lori arrived, she lit up her first cigarette. The three of us sat at the kitchen table while Lori plunged into the latest story about what she had heard Dan was doing with other women *this* week. While she lit cigarette after cigarette, Sarah watched the white roll of tobacco go from her lips to the coffee cup saucer she used as an ashtray, and back to her lips. Sarah appeared shocked when Lori told us she drank a whole six-pack of beer by herself the night before.

I calmly said, "What triggered that response, Lori?"

She responded, "I'm tired of being alone and I'm tired of playing the role of a convenient weekend toy."

"What do you mean?" I inquired.

She told us that for the past ten years, she'd had an annual weekend getaway with a man she dated in college. She said it all started when he called one day and asked her to meet him at an out-of-state location where he was on a business trip. Even though she was married, she made an excuse to her husband and took a flight to meet her ex-boyfriend.

"We *always* have a good time. We *always* sleep together. We *always* say we wish we had married each other. But he *never* says he'll leave his wife and marry me. I feel like I'm a useless plaything. I'm hurt and I'm mad. Aren't I good enough for *anybody* to love?"

When I told Lori that I'd been praying for her every day, she said, "You *have? Why* would you do that? My life isn't *worth* being prayed for."

I had shared part of my testimony with her, and Lori knew I was "a religious person," as she put it. But this afternoon I was able to tell her the story of the woman at the well and Jesus' response to this woman who felt forsaken by a series of men. I explained the love Christ had for her and the difference He had made in my life. Lori didn't accept the Lord that day, but as she left, Sarah and I knew God had used this encounter to get her to think about God's unconditional love.

After Lori's departure, Sarah looked at me and said, "I watched you today while you invited Lori into your home. You let her smoke in your kitchen. You listened to her tell about a ten-year affair. She cussed a lot, and she's not someone I would enjoy spending much time with, but I saw you make her feel valued . . . to feel cared for. I know she listened when we talked about God because she first knew that you accepted and loved her as a person. I really don't have any nonChristian friends, but I saw today that if I don't build relationships with people who need to know God's love, I probably won't get to be the one who introduces them to Christ." That afternoon provided me with a unique opportunity to show unconditional love to Lori, but it also allowed me to positively influence Sarah's life with new ideas on how to reach the people around her for Christ.

CONTEMPORARY APPLICATIONS OF JESUS' TEACHINGS

Here are some other ways of mentoring through the principle of unconditional love:

When someone with whom you are in a mentoring relationship becomes upset with you, stop and realize that person probably misunderstood you. Ask God to reveal anything wrong on your part that needs an apology. Take action, if necessary. If there's nothing to apologize for, forgive her anyway — first in your heart, and then by doing a conscious act of kindness for her.

Introduce women you are seeking to influence to the idea of doing acts of kindness to demonstrate Christ's love. I recently had a woman with me when I purchased a "Veggie Tales" video for another woman who does child-care in her home. This woman had recently lost her mother to cancer and felt discouraged. We stopped by her home with our surprise. You would have thought we had brought her a dozen roses. She hugged both of us as she said, "It's good to know somebody loves me and understands what I've been going through lately." Afterward, the young friend who was with me said, "Wow! It makes me want to think up one thing a day that will touch the lives of people with Jesus' love. It's so much fun!"

LETTING GOD LOVE YOU

You might be struggling with the idea of loving others unconditionally because you feel that you have never been loved that way yourself. You know the amazing story of the ultimate price Jesus paid to demonstrate His unconditional love for you, but practicing the *giving* and *receiving* of His love on a daily basis is sometimes challenging.

This is an excellent issue to address in your time alone with God. Ask God to help you experience His love. If we are lovable to God — so lovable that He sacrificed His own Son for us — that means we are women of significance, honor, and great worth. That sense of security should give us the confidence to begin giving unconditional love to others.

1. When in your life have you been loved unconditionally? (Or, what's the closest thing to unconditional love that you've experienced?)

2. *The Message* translates 1 Corinthians 13:4-7 like this:

> *Love doesn't strut,*
> *Doesn't have a swelled head,*
> *Doesn't force itself on others,*
> *Isn't always "me first,"*
> *Doesn't fly off the handle,*
> *Doesn't keep score of the sins of others,*
> *Doesn't revel when others grovel,*
> *Takes pleasure in the flowering of truth,*
> *Puts up with anything,*
> *Trusts God always,*
> *Always looks for the best,*
> *Never looks back,*
> *But keeps going to the end.*

Which three or four things in that list are most important to you when you receive love from someone?

3. Read the story of the Samaritan woman in John 4:1-28.

a. What made this woman such an outcast?

b. What are some things that cause women in today's culture to feel rejected and unloved?

c. The following are paraphrases of the Samaritan woman's questions and statements. How did Jesus respond to each one?

• But I'm the wrong nationality.

• How can you get living water when you don't even have a bucket?

• I don't have a husband.

• You're Jewish, so you think Jerusalem is the only place for worship, right?

4. Read John 4:39-42. What was the end result of the unconditional love Jesus gave to the Samaritan woman?

5. Review the three important stages in loving someone else according to John Powell (page 79). Why do you think a challenge to action is stage 3 instead of stage 1? (Why is it included at all?)

6. Have you ever had trouble showing unconditional love? What has God taught you about that situation?

7. Read Matthew 5:44-48.

a. Summarize the instructions Jesus gives on loving people who are unlovable.

b. What objections might someone raise to these instructions?

c. What do you think Jesus would say in response to those objections?

8. How easy is it for you to let God love you on a daily basis? Why do you suppose that is?

9. How can the group pray for you this week?

When the group is ready to pray, have everyone close her eyes while one person reads aloud the following verses:

> *This is how much God loved the world: He gave his Son, his one and only Son. And this is why: so that no one need be destroyed; by believing in him, anyone can have a whole and lasting life. God didn't go to all the trouble of sending his Son merely to point an accusing finger, telling the world how bad it was. He came to help, to put the world right again. (John 3:16-17)*

> *The* LORD *appeared to us in the past, saying: "I have loved you with an everlasting love; I have drawn you with unfailing kindness." (Jeremiah 31:3, NIV)*

Begin your time of prayer by telling God how you respond to His gift of unconditional love.

chapter seven

the principle of casting vision

ay was the first adult outside my family who told me I had potential to do something great for God. He was the state director of Youth for Christ. When I got home after my first year of college, Ray asked if I would join a teen team for the summer with five other university students. I accepted. We performed upbeat, contemporary music that attracted crowds on a beach, at a county fair, or in a city park. We approached people after our free concerts with a booklet called "The Balanced Life Quiz." Our purpose was to introduce people to Christ after leading them through the key questions in the quiz.

I enjoyed this opportunity at first, but soon there was a major wrinkle. All of the other team members had been in international touring music groups and their musical talents were enviable. We had two trombonists, a trumpeter, a flutist, and a keyboard artist, and all of them could solo on the vocals, as well as with their instruments. The audience would shout out the name of a popular song and these people could play it flawlessly — in any key, without sheet music — and do stylistic variations within the piece, from jazz to country, or classical to calypso.

I was out of my league musically and felt miserable. In spite of my desire to invest my summer in something of lasting value, I knew I didn't fit. Ray sensed my uneasiness and pulled me aside. I told him I loved being on the team, but I didn't want to hurt the group's musical reputation. Ray looked me in the eyes and said, "Carol, the reason we brought this team together is that there are so many teenagers in this area who need Christ. You have an ability to relate to them. The team we've put together has incredible musical talent, but you have *personality*!"

He went on: "Carol, our main purpose is to introduce teenagers to personal faith in Christ, and your contribution to the team is outstanding. You concisely introduce the songs and tell humorous stories that keep people laughing and listening. And when you mingle in the crowd afterward, it's awesome to see how people relate to you. They actually cluster around while you are telling them how to establish a meaningful relationship with Christ. You have a remarkable gift of evangelism."

When Ray finished, my self-esteem was intact. He made me believe I had something worthwhile to contribute to the team's ministry and that I was not only *needed*, but *wanted*. When he established that my main function on the team was *personality*, the rest of the team applauded my gifts. All of us understood our individual purposes.

I recently wrote down how Ray's visionary leadership had influenced me:

He made me feel valuable. By affirming my strength (personality) and my spiritual gift (evangelism), he helped me realize I made an essential contribution to the team.

He painted a clear picture of our mission and my contribution. I finally understood that our goal was not to do professional concerts. Our goal was evangelism, and my place on the team was key if we were going to fulfill our purpose.

He set me up for success, not failure. He freed me from having to do something I wasn't good at, and encouraged me to do what I could do best — meet people and tell them about Jesus.

He inspired me. I felt privileged to communicate truth to people who needed a fresh touch from God in their lives. I knew there was nothing more important to do with my time and energy. This was *kingdom work!*

He gave enough training to make us feel prepared, but enough freedom to help us accomplish the mission in creative, contemporary ways. Community Bible study teaching director Margaret Frost says, "People are encouraged to become their best when you hold a crown just a little above their heads and ask them to grow into it."[1] That's what Ray did. Our team had the freedom to evaluate each new audience and make changes if we believed a variation in our regular program would reach a particular group more effectively. When we made a mistake or failed, he was there to help us try again. He coached us and affirmed us through the process.

Most individuals do not think they are *special* enough to make a difference. We need to affirm our belief in their ability to change the world with their unique gifts. When we do, we are following Jesus' example.

Jesus ignited His disciples' hearts with God's vision for redeeming this world. Pastor Bill Hybels speculates that Jesus must have thought, "I can continue to do everything, or I can build the leadership abilities of people who can take the baton when I return to the Father."[2] Hybels continues, "When you have an exciting, God-inspired vision and you invite others to help bring that vision to life, most will be grateful that you asked for their help. . . . Jesus concerned Himself with far more than preaching and healing — He invested heavily in developing the people who were following Him."[3]

How did Jesus ignite a vision within His disciples' hearts?

JESUS SAW PEOPLE'S POTENTIAL

Jesus had an amazing ability to look at people and see their God-given potential. He took unlikely candidates — fishermen and tax collectors — who were not about to attach themselves to rabbinic schools and turned them into His dedicated disciples.

When I pray about who God wants me to mentor intentionally, I ask that I would be able to look past the woman's current ministry position and past her education (or lack of it) and see her potential. Perhaps she doesn't look like it today, but she may be the next Henrietta Mears or Corrie ten Boom or Elisabeth Elliot. We need to ask God to give us lenses through which we can see the potential of the people around us, to quicken our mind and touch our spirit with discernment as we invest time and training in them.

JESUS GAVE THEM A VISION OF WHAT THEY COULD DO

After Peter recognized that Jesus was the Christ, the Messiah, the Son of the living God, Jesus said to him,

> *My Father in heaven, God himself, let you in on this secret of who I really am. And now I'm going to tell you who you are, really are. You are Peter, a rock. This is the rock on which I will put together my church, a church so expansive with energy that not even the gates of hell will be able to keep it out. And that's not all. You will have complete and free access to God's kingdom, keys to open any and every door: no more barriers between heaven and earth, earth and heaven. (Matthew 16:17-19)*

Talk about building confidence in a person and casting a vision!

When we work with people and name the potential we see in them, it helps them to envision their personal worth to God and to us:

- "Susan, you have great administrative ability."
- "Kathy, you have a unique ability to negotiate peace in the middle of dissenting opinions on the women's ministries team."
- "Jan, when you led us in prayer at our last committee meeting, God used you to create an atmosphere of unity and spiritual oneness."
- "Heather, you have a remarkable ability to make the Bible study lectures come alive. You are an outstanding researcher and you have a gift for teaching."

We have to be careful about jumping to conclusions when we affirm people regarding their God-given potential, but our prayerful words about what we see in others helps give them a vision of what their future ministry might be.

JESUS PREPARED HIS FOLLOWERS FOR WHAT TO EXPECT

In Matthew 10, Jesus gave His followers some very specific instructions:

Start where you are with what you see. "It's best to start small. Give a cool cup of water to someone who is thirsty, for instance" (verse 42).

"Do not go among the Gentiles. . . ." It wasn't that He didn't care about the Gentiles, but because no foundational work had been done with them, He knew He would be setting His disciples up for failure if they went there with no experience (verse 5, NIV).

There will be times when people are unresponsive and your ministry has no fruit. Don't get "all beaten up" over that; expect it and move on. "When you knock on a door, be courteous in your greeting. If they welcome you, be gentle in your conversation. If they don't welcome you, quietly withdraw. Don't make a scene. Shrug your shoulders and be on your way" (verses 12-14).

You are not alone in this great work. "We are intimately linked in this harvest work. Anyone who accepts what you do, accepts me, the One who sent you. Anyone who accepts what I do accepts my Father, who sent me" (verse 40).

Find your niche in My plan. No function is greater than another. "The smallest act of giving or receiving makes you a true apprentice. You won't lose out on a thing" (verse 42).

JESUS GAVE THEM A CHALLENGING, VISIONARY TASK

After His resurrection, Jesus appeared to the Eleven as they were eating supper and said, "Go into the world. Go everywhere and announce the Message of God's good news to one and all" (Mark 16:15). That was a massive, extraordinary challenge! Yet we know the disciples succeeded. The vision of Christ is still being carried on today. If we follow Christ's example, we will mobilize a future generation of people who will live out their purpose.

Several years ago, I led a home Bible study to help women get prepared to share their faith. Some weeks into the study, I challenged the women to talk about their faith with someone God put in their path the following week. I told them I would take on the same challenge and we would report back at the next Bible study about what happened.

I left for a four-day insurance convention with my husband. One morning Gene had a business meeting and I had a free morning. I walked back into my hotel room after enjoying an early walk on the beach, and the maid was there. She had finished cleaning the bathroom and was about to put clean sheets on the bed. I greeted her warmly and said, "I'd like to help you make the bed."

With an incredulous look, she said, "Why, thank you, Ma'am. I've worked at this hotel for five years and no one has ever done that before."

As we pulled the bedspread over the pillows, I asked her about her family. She was a single mom raising two small children on a limited income. Life was hard, and she was struggling to make ends meet. As she finished up in the room, I had the perfect opportunity to tell her about my faith in Jesus Christ. She hung on every word. And at the end of our time together, she prayed to receive Christ. I took her address, hugged her goodbye, and promised to be in touch with her by mail.

At our next Bible study, all the group could talk about were the exciting encounters they had with people the previous week. Sally talked to her hairdresser about an answer to prayer. Bonnie asked her neighbor over for coffee and shared her testimony at the kitchen table. Jean had a unique opportunity to voice her faith with her son's third-grade teacher. One after the other, they told of the ways God opened doors for them to "announce the message of God's good news."

I told them what happened when I presented the gospel to the maid in South Carolina, and they wanted to drop everything and pray for this young woman and her children. This one-week "experiment" provided a momentum that continued to grow throughout the rest of the Bible study and beyond. They caught the vision.

RESTORING HOPE AND COURAGE

Martha Strickland is the former director of training and education for CBInternational, a Christian mission organization. She met her mentor, Dr. Paula Martinez, when she was a student at Wheaton College. Martha describes a professor who gave her a vision of her purpose:

> She was the first professor who took a personal interest in me. She spent hours coaching and affirming me in my quest as a new teacher. During the spring semester she chose me to be her first teacher's assistant. Even in that position, I was not just given the "grunge" duties, like photocopying and simple clerical work. She trusted me to work on her postdoctoral research.
>
> After I graduated, she kept in contact and supported me as I went overseas as a teacher. I came back on my first furlough exhausted, broken, and doubting my future as a teacher. I called Dr. Martinez and after hearing my shaky voice, she cleared her schedule and picked me up for lunch the next day. She gave me the gift of a listening ear as I poured out my struggles. Then she surprised me by taking me to the classroom of a master teacher in the area. She deposited me at the door, talked to the teacher, and left.

I sat in that classroom and watched this master teacher at work for hours. I saw her use the same methods I had used in the mission school; I realized her challenges in the classroom matched some of those I had faced. I entered that classroom weary, broken, and full of self-doubt, but I left with renewed hope. I am so grateful for a mentor who helped me to recover my lost vision and gave me the courage to keep pioneering in new areas of education.

Dr. Paula Martinez demonstrates the importance of casting vision during the inevitable times when those we mentor experience failure. Good mentors restore hope, courage, and the ability to see a better future.

WHAT HAPPENS WHEN YOU ACT ON GOD'S VISION FOR YOUR LIFE?

What happens when you catch a vision of what God might be doing in your life and then you act on that dream?

You experience *risk.* In 1983 I gave up the most meaningful Christian ministry I'd ever been involved in — teaching Bible Study Fellowship classes. I couldn't do that and follow the new direction I sensed from God: to launch a training seminar for women who wanted to learn how to communicate effectively. When I left my job as the teaching leader, I felt I was risking the possibility of giving up my sense of spiritual fulfillment.

You experience *fear.* The Enemy approached me with hundreds of reasons why I could never be qualified to teach a group of women how to speak. *Who did I think I was?* For a while I wondered if launching this communications seminar was just an ego trip that would wind up making me feel like an idiot.

You experience *total dependence on God.* When you start feeling weak, you start seeking His face through prayer and Bible study. The more I prayed, the more I felt an urgency to use my gifts to train others in how to speak. The more I read the Bible, the more

God confirmed through Scripture that I was following His visionary will for my life in launching this seminar.

You experience *joy*. There can be no greater joy than living out your purpose. As I moved forward in the direction in which God had been pointing my vision, I sensed the joy of "living in the smile of God's approval."

You receive *more assignments*. The Christian life is never static. As God confirms your vision, new doors open. Current tasks are delegated to people who are ready to risk saying "yes" to Him. And "creative restlessness" returns. But this time, you know it's the Holy Spirit saying, "Listen up! I have another demanding but fulfilling task for you to do."

WILL YOU JOIN THE ADVENTURE?

If we want to impact lives as Jesus did, we will give people opportunities to grow, and then encourage and help them if they fail. It means taking the time to pray with them, train them, and encourage them. Sometimes it means watching them fail the first time they try a new task. Author and speaker Jan Johnson writes, "When pondering dreams, many conclude: *I could never do this. . . . I'm not clever enough . . . it'll never succeed. . . .* But failure is normal, even essential. It is the fertile ground from which success arises. . . . The question is not whether you've made some mistakes or failed in the past, but whether you'll let fear keep you from trying."[4]

Let's not let fear hold us back. Let's see people as Jesus saw them — people with great potential. Remember, making a lasting impact on others doesn't have to do with *you*, it has to do with how much you become like *Jesus*. If you and I want to become women of influence, we will do what Jesus did.

1. Spend time alone with God.
2. Walk and talk with people so that we can influence them through impact moments.

3. Ask people questions, especially ones that don't have "yes" or "no" answers.
4. Show compassion.
5. Practice unconditional love.
6. Cast the vision of what Jesus can do through the life of someone who is willing to give her potential to Him.

Author and speaker Os Guinness might have said it best:

> Do you have a reason for being, a focused sense of purpose in your life? Or is your life the product of shifting resolutions and the myriad pull of forces outside yourself? Do you want to go beyond success to significance? Have you come to realize that self-reliance always falls short and that world-denying solutions provide no answer in the end? Listen to Jesus of Nazareth; answer His call.[5]

1. Who was the first person outside of your family who made you feel you could do something great with your life? What did that person do?

2. In this chapter's opening story on pages 91-92, how did Ray help Carol get a vision of what God could do through her?

3. Read Matthew 10:39-42.

a. Jesus prepared His followers for what to expect when they became His disciples. What advice and encouragement did He give?

b. How is this advice relevant to your situation?

4. Read Mark 16:15.

a. How do you think Jesus' instruction to His disciples applies to you today?

b. What goes through your mind when you think about following that vision?

5. Review Martha Strickland's story on pages 97-98.

    a. How did Dr. Paula Martinez cast vision for Martha?

    b. When have you needed that kind of mentoring?

6. Take a few minutes on your own to reflect on the vision God has given you for your life. Maybe you see only a tiny step — that's okay! What do you already know or suspect about what God wants to do through you? Jot some notes to focus your thoughts.

I think God is calling me to

What I want to ask God is

7. How can the group support you in prayer to follow God's vision for your life? If you like, you can begin your time of prayer by having someone read aloud the following:

> *Lord, I'm available. Reveal Your vision to me. I am no longer content to live a safe Christian life. Move me out of my comfort zone. I long for an adventure in trusting You. I hang my weakness on Your strength. I want to live out the principles Jesus modeled. I want to be a woman of influence who is making a lasting impact on others. Amen.*

What's the next step for your group? Consider a celebration to mark the end of this study and the launch of the next stage of your journey.

notes

CHAPTER TWO

1. Richard Foster, *Celebration of Discipline* (San Francisco: Harper & Row, 1978), pp. 84-85.

CHAPTER FOUR

1. Robert C. Crosby and Pamela Crosby, "Now That's a Good Question," *Focus on the Family,* December 1996, p. 7.
2. Todd Catteau, "The Questions of Jesus," *Discipleship Journal,* No. 10, July/August 1997, p. 24.
3. Hebrews 13:5b, NIV

CHAPTER FIVE

1. Spiros Zodhiates, *The Complete Word Study Dictionary* (Chattanooga, Tenn.: AMG Publishers, 1992), p. 1,306.
2. Jess Moody, as quoted by Lloyd Cory, *Quotable Quotations* (Wheaton, Ill.: Victor, 1985), p. 76.
3. Corrie ten Boom, *Clippings from My Notebook* (Minneapolis, Minn.: World Wide, 1982), p. 115.

CHAPTER SIX

1. *The Quest Study Bible* (Grand Rapids, Mich.: Zondervan, 1994), p. 1471.
2. John Powell, *Unconditional Love* (Niles, Ill.: Argus Communications, 1978), pp. 83-84.
3. Billy Graham as quoted by Lloyd Cory, *Quotable Quotations* (Wheaton, Ill.: Victor, 1985), p. 226.

CHAPTER SEVEN

1. Quote contributed by Carol John from a Bible study lecture by Margaret Frost.
2. Bill Hybels, "Lead, Manage, Shepherd, Teach," from the "Defining Moments, Legacy of a Leader" tape series.
3. Hybels, 43, pp. 1-2.
4. Jan Johnson, "What If I Fail?" *Virtue Magazine*, May/June 1994, p. 46.
5. Os Guinness, *The Call* (Nashville, Tenn.: Word, 1998), p. 7.

Increasing Your Influence Is Simple As 1, 2, 3!

It's easy to begin a self-improvement program,

but it's really hard to stay with it! At *Thrive!*, we fully understand

that to achieve continuous, sustainable personal growth

we all need help.

That's why we've developed this simple-to-follow,

three-step program to increase your personal influence.

We firmly believe in your potential as a leader and

we want to provide you the best quality leadership resources.

Prepare to take three giants steps toward

Becoming a Woman of Influence!

Step 1

Visit us at **www.BecomingaWomanofInfluence.com** and receive your FREE audio copy of *Increasing Your Influence*. This is a leadership lesson by John C. Maxwell to help you take the next step in your personal development program. *Increasing Your Influence* is available to you either online in streaming audio format or if you would prefer to add this lesson to your personal leadership library, we can ship you a copy on either audiocassette or CD for a minimal shipping charge of $2.00.

THRIVE!
Becoming a Woman of Influence
www.INJOY.com/Thrive

Step 2

Subscribe to *Thrive! Today*. This innovative influence-building audio magazine for women, delivered right to your door on a monthly basis, provides hours of ongoing personal mentoring from some of the most influential female leaders in the church and business community. Call **1-800-333-6506** to subscribe today.

Step 3

Practice what you're learning by influencing others! We can help you begin the challenging and rewarding process of extending yourself to others by providing a host of additional resources. *The Becoming a Person of Influence* video kit series is an ideal place to begin in a small group environment. Order your kit today at **www.INJOY.com!**